Quilting Design
SOURCEBOOK

Dorothy Osler

That
Patchwork
Place®

Acknowledgements

I must thank Katy Lewis of Caerphilly, South Wales, for permission to reproduce her pattern Abertridwr Star, and Narelle Grieve of New South Wales, Australia, for bringing to my attention her wonderful whole-cloth quilt with Mrs. Boundy's Tulip upon it.

I must also thank my students, past and present, for the stimulus of ideas generated and problems discussed. In many ways, this book is a response to their comments and concerns in choosing patterns and planning designs for quilting.

I am indebted to Aidan Nichol for technical help. To my husband, Adrian Osler, I must again give my heartfelt thanks for his constant support and belief in my ability to "get there."

Library of Congress Cataloging-in-Publication Data

Osler, Dorothy.
    Quilting design sourcebook / Dorothy Osler.
       p.   cm.
    Includes bibliographical references and index.
    ISBN 1-56477-152-0
    1. Quilting —Patterns. 2. Quilts—Design. I. Title.
TT835.085 1996   96-16464
746.46'041—dc20   CIP

Credits

Editorial Director . . . . Kerry I. Hoffman
Technical Editor . . . . Sharon Rose
Copy Editor . . . . Liz McGehee
Proofreader . . . . Melissa Riesland
Illustrators . . . . Laurel Strand, Carolyn Kraft, Bruce Stout
Photographer . . . . Brent Kane
Design Director . . . . Judy Petry
Text and Cover Designer . . . . Kay Green
Production Assistant . . . . Shean Bemis

Quilting Design Sourcebook
©1996 by Dorothy Osler

That Patchwork Place, Inc.
PO Box 118
Bothell, WA 98041-0118 USA

Printed in Hong Kong
01 00 99 98 97 96 6 5 4 3 2 1

MISSION STATEMENT

WE ARE DEDICATED TO PROVIDING QUALITY PRODUCTS AND SERVICES THAT INSPIRE CREATIVITY. WE WORK TOGETHER TO ENRICH THE LIVES WE TOUCH. *That Patchwork Place is a financially responsible ESOP company.*

Contents

Introduction

I come from a part of the world—Northeast England—where quiltmaking has long been part of traditional culture. In that tradition, the quilting itself (as opposed to piecing) held the most interest. Whether the quilts were pieced or appliquéd, whole-cloth or "strippy" (like bar quilts), they were heavily quilted in a distinctive style and with characteristic patterns.

I have to confess that my own introduction to quiltmaking was not through these traditional quilts of my native Northeast England. My introduction, like that of so many quilters world-wide, was through American quilts and quilters. We have learned the techniques and the language of quiltmaking under the influence and vitality of the dynamic American tradition and within the context of the late-twentieth-century quilt revival. We have adapted to new materials and tools, and developed wonderful skills. Now the world of quilting moves on as a global and interactive one.

As I immersed myself more and more in quiltmaking, it became impossible to ignore the traditions of my region. I was shown old quilts and told about past quilters, and I eventually discovered a generation of professional quiltmakers and designers that had prospered from the 1860s to the 1930s. Then I looked farther afield at the quilts of Britain as a whole, for it is a fact that many British quilts have wonderful quilting designs on them.

I have spent many years looking at old quilts and learning to "read" the quilting designs and patterns on them. One fact has become plain: the patterns on old quilts show a knowledge of quilting design that has not yet been improved upon.

Looking at old quilts, I noticed the same pattern appeared on one quilt looking insipid and lifeless, but on another quilt, it had beauty and movement. Why was this? In some cases, the quality of the pattern was at fault. Some patterns were simply badly drawn or badly proportioned. Squat and ugly feather patterns do nothing for a quilt's design.

But it's not just the pattern itself that works or doesn't work well in a design. It's also the way the pattern is used—how it's presented, oriented, and combined with other pattern units in the design—that makes it look good.

The quilters whose work I most admired knew how to modify and combine patterns for best effect. Variation and combination are the twin threads running through this book. Exciting things can happen when you play with patterns. Change a line here, add a line there, fill a space. Then combine two or three (or more) patterns and see what happens. It can be every bit as much fun as playing with shapes for piecing.

Unfortunately, our standards for quilting design tend to be lower than those for piecing and appliqué. All too often, stencils are purchased and placed on quilts—in setting blocks, corners, or borders—with little thought to how the pattern can be adapted or linked into a co-ordinated design.

My real dream is for quilters to approach quilting design with the same energy and skill that go into other aspects of quiltmaking, and to rediscover what well-planned and well-stitched quilting patterns can contribute to surface quilt design.

In assembling my library of quilting patterns, I have drawn on a variety of sources. Some patterns are traditional, some are ancient decorative motifs, and some are original ideas. These patterns are both appealing and suitable for quilting. They can be used on quilts large and small, and also for smaller items such as pillows and wall hangings.

Before looking at the pattern library in detail, let's consider some basics of quilting design.

Quilting Design

Design, like sewing, is a learned skill. And like sewing, design improves with experience and know-how. There are techniques to be learned and practised for quilting design, just as there are techniques for using colour and shape in pieced quilts. With practice comes confidence, energy, and the skills to try out new ideas and develop new techniques.

To help you understand the basic principles of using quilting patterns, the following sections consider those patterns' nature and characteristics.

PATTERNS

Quilting patterns are the building blocks for design. The way individual patterns are put together makes the quilting design. In other words, quilting patterns fit together in a planned combination or layout to create a quilting design. And how well those patterns are put together determines the quality of the design.

Quilting patterns fall into three basic groups:

Motifs. These self-contained patterns can "stand alone" or be combined in groups. All the patterns in this book are motifs.

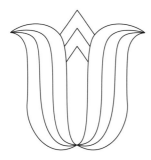

Filler patterns. These patterns fill the spaces in or around motifs. (See page 93.)

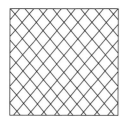

Border patterns. These patterns link together to frame areas of the quilt surface. Some border patterns are special linking or overlapping patterns, such as braids. Others are simply arrangements of motifs and filler patterns.

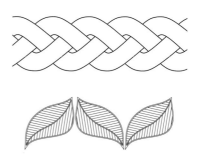

"COLOUR"

The quilting design on the surface of any quilt is defined by lines of stitching. If those lines are close together, the quilt layers are compressed and visually recede on the quilt surface. We can think of this as negative, dark, or receding space. If, however, the quilt lines are farther apart, the batting lofts up in between to create positive, light, or raised space on the quilt surface.

Creating contrast over the quilt surface by developing both raised areas and denser areas can help make a good quilting design. It is a bit like using light- and dark-toned fabrics in pieced designs. Using contrast in this way brings "colour" to your quilting design.

It is not difficult to work contrast into your design. It is a matter of how you use motifs and filler patterns together. As a general rule, motifs are used as the light, raised areas of the quilt surface, and filler patterns represent the darker, receding areas. Whole-cloth quilts, in particular, need contrast to create interest on the quilt surface and to prevent patterns from becoming an indistinguishable blur.

If you want contrast, think carefully about the line spacing of your motifs and filler patterns. If the lines are equally spaced, the design will contain no positive or negative space and will appear flat.

Choose closer line spacing for your filler pattern to solve this.

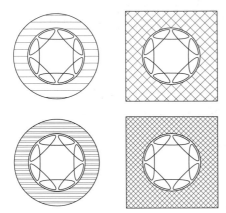

It is possible to create contrast within, as well as around, a motif. If you use filler patterns within a motif, those areas become negative space. This aspect of pattern variation will be discussed in more detail in the next chapter. (See page 8.)

SYMMETRY

Symmetrical patterns can be divided by imaginary lines into equal, mirror-image segments. Some motifs are symmetrical, but many are not. Symmetry does not make a pattern any more exciting, but it is a factor to consider when planning a design. Symmetry may help you combine patterns or fit groups of the same motif together.

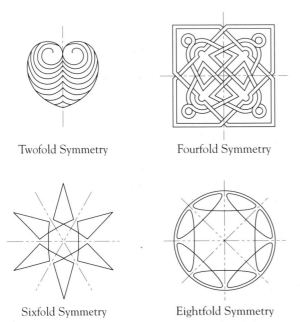

Twofold Symmetry   Fourfold Symmetry

Sixfold Symmetry   Eightfold Symmetry

Some motifs within these pages are symmetrical; others are asymmetrical. Circles and stars have a basic symmetry: fourfold, sixfold, or eightfold. Most patterns drawn from nature (flowers, feathers) are asymmetrical.

As a simple exercise, look through the "Pattern Library" on pages 11–80 and work out the symmetry of each pattern.

SPACE

All the motifs in the "Pattern Library" have been chosen for their attractiveness as decorative units. But one element frequently overlooked is the space between motifs. It is possible to combine motifs in such a way that the space in between becomes as eye-catching, or even more so, than the motifs themselves.

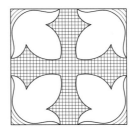 

Welsh Tulip pattern appears on page 64.

Fan pattern appears on page 46.

STYLE

Many decorative patterns have an intrinsic style—the result of the gradual evolution of a form in a certain time or place. In the world of quilting, the distinctive piecing style of the Seminole Indians, the colourful Hawaiian appliqué quilts, and the elegant Japanese Sashiko style of quilting all spring to mind. English North Country quilting includes patterns that are curvilinear and often have scalloped outlines. Celtic patterns have a distinctive interwoven style.

Be alert to style when mixing different patterns, or the result may be a hotchpotch of styles that do not blend. Put another way, to achieve a certain style within your design, choose patterns that represent that style.

How to Use the Patterns

The following are some techniques for varying and combining the full-scale patterns in the "Pattern Library." Alternatively, you may wish to use the basic motifs or one of the variations just as they are and quilt them into setting blocks or pillow tops.

REORIENTING

Full-scale patterns can be repositioned or reoriented in different ways. Look closely at the pattern symmetry. If the motif has a fourfold, sixfold, or eightfold symmetry, it can be reoriented. Rotate a motif with fourfold symmetry by 45°, one with sixfold symmetry by 30°, and one with eightfold symmetry by 22½°, and notice the difference it makes. Remember that rotating a motif can change the amount of space it occupies.

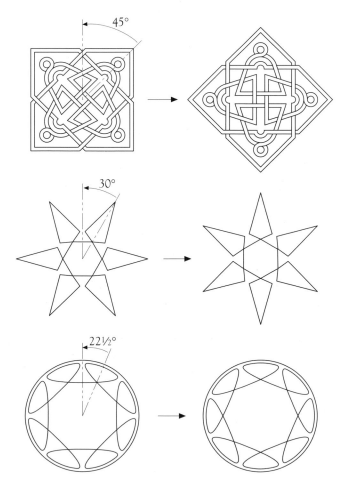

Asymmetrical motifs can also be reoriented. For example, take the Goosewing pattern on page 44. The angle at which border motifs are placed determines both the look of the design and the amount of space it takes up.

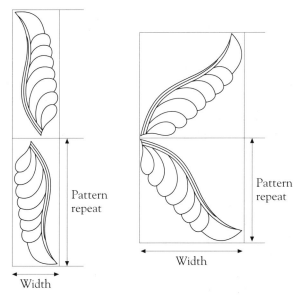

ENLARGING AND REDUCING

You may find that the motif in the book is too large or too small for your needs. If so, use a photocopier to enlarge or reduce the pattern. You may photocopy the designs for your personal use.

Most of the motifs in this book fit into an 8" x 8" block. Enlargements/reductions for other standard block sizes are given in the box on page 11. To calculate the percentage of enlargement or reduction for other sizes, divide the size of the block or space you want to fill by the original pattern size. If the full-scale pattern fits into an 8" block, and your space is 11" x 11", divide 11 by 8. The result (in this case 1.375) is the proportion by which you need to enlarge the full-scale pattern (137.5%). For a 4" block, divide 4 by 8 to get .5, or a 50% reduction. When figuring your sizes, don't forget to take into account whether the block will be set straight or on point. (See page 11.)

VARYING

Any quilting pattern can be varied in some way; some patterns can be varied in many ways. To begin this process, many of the motifs are presented with two variations. Other variations are possible, so once you have mastered the simple techniques behind pattern variation, try your own ideas.

Double Lining

One of the simplest ways to vary a pattern is to outline the motif. This technique is known as double lining and was often used by traditional hand quilters. They understood the simple principle that double lining adds greater emphasis to the motif and separates it more clearly from the surrounding filler pattern. Double lines are usually stitched ¼" from the outer edge of the pattern. Remember that double lining will increase the size of the motif.

¼" or less, depending on size of pattern

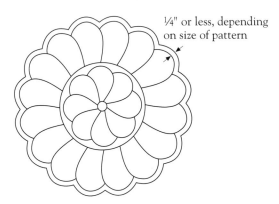

Double lining Rose in a Ring sharpens the motif and provides a containing frame, setting it apart from any surrounding filler pattern.

Another line can be added—called "triple lining"—but this can overpower a pattern and detract from its quality.

Fillers

Another simple technique for varying patterns is adding areas of filler pattern inside the motif. This creates zones of negative space inside the motif. Filler patterns can be geometric (single or double line) or random (stipple quilting or meander quilting). (See page 93.)

Echo filling is the term used to describe parallel quilting lines that follow the outline of the space you are filling.

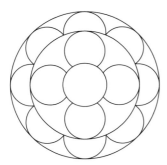

Echo filling selected areas of the Scalloped Circle and rotating it transforms the pattern into a cruciform version with elegance and depth.

ADAPTING

Motifs can also be changed by adding or removing lines inside the motif or by doubling particular lines. This alters the internal line structure of the motif, so care must be taken not to inadvertently change the pattern symmetry.

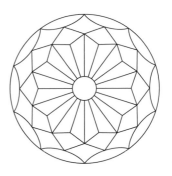

Adapting the internal lines of the Faceted Circle, rotating it, then adding a filler pattern dramatically modifies the central zone of the pattern.

COMBINING

Repeats of the same motif can be linked together and set in simple combinations—pairs, radial groups, or chains. Indeed, motifs that have a strong visual style of their own—for example, Celtic and feather patterns—are better left as is and used singly or in combinations. Too much variation on such patterns can destroy their intrinsic style.

Ideas for combining patterns are given for those motifs that work particularly well in groups.

Mirror-Image Pairs

Two motifs may be arranged in a mirror-image pair. These pairs can be linked for borders or used in radial groups and chains. To create a mirror image, you must flip the pattern.

Mirror-Image Pair

To mark a mirror-image pattern, photocopy the original, then turn it over and affix it to a light box or bright window. Lay the fabric over the photocopy, secure, and trace.

Another option is to trace the pattern onto template plastic, then use the plastic to make a stencil or outline template. (See "Marking" on page 88.) Use the pattern right side up for one of the images and right side down for the mirror image.

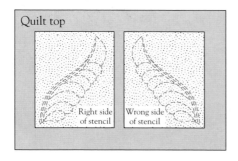

When fitting mirror-image pairs into spaces on your quilt, treat each pair as a unit, not as two separate patterns. Measure the length of the pair, taking into account the orientation you plan to use and the amount of space you need between the two images. Make sure you have enough space for repeats.

Radial Groups

Radial groups of motifs are particularly suitable for quilt centres and setting blocks. Motifs are usually combined in symmetrical groups of four, six, or eight, although other combinations are possible.

In a fourfold arrangement, motifs need to be 90° apart; in a sixfold arrangement, 60° apart; and in an eightfold arrangement, 45° apart. To position and mark motifs in radial groups, use a large quilters' ruler to maintain the correct angles and positions.

Chains

Chains of motifs can frame either large or small areas of the quilt surface. Chains are most often used in borders, but smaller chains can also be used around quilt centres, where they act as separators, creating barriers between different elements of the quilting pattern and producing a much tidier design. Chains can also be used in setting strips or to separate quilting patterns in a whole-cloth quilted sampler.

To form a chain, a motif needs to have linkage points. Stars make good chains, as do other motifs with projecting points, such as leaves and flowers.

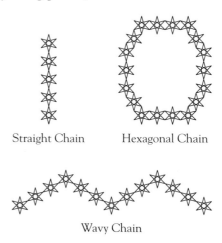

Straight Chain   Hexagonal Chain

Wavy Chain

Some motifs in a chain may need to be reoriented. In the border chain of fans on page 47, every other motif is turned 180°. This gives the combination a swirling movement, producing a wavy chain.

Pattern Library

Before you begin, take note of the following:

- Block sizes and border lengths given *do not* include seam allowances. Add ¼"-wide seam allowances in all cases.
- Pattern sizes, block sizes, and border lengths are dimensions before quilting. Quilting causes shrinkage, the extent of which depends on your design and the batting you use. Close quilting and thicker batting cause more shrinkage than open quilting and thinner batting.
- When you choose quilting patterns, remember that some motifs—for example, circular ones like the Breton Fisherman's Knot below—will take up the same amount of space whether the block is set straight or on point; other motifs will take up more or less space. This information is provided with relevant motifs.

- Most motifs in the library are accompanied by two half-scale variations. To use the variations, photocopy the full-scale pattern and add or remove lines using the variation diagram as a guide. Alternatively, you could enlarge the variations and trace from your enlargement. Follow the instructions on page 7 for calculating the percentage.

Unless otherwise noted, full-scale motifs will fit inside an 8" x 8" block set straight or on point. Enlarge or reduce as indicated for the following block sizes:

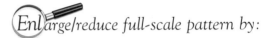

Enlarge/reduce full-scale pattern by:

6" x 6" block: 75%
10" x 10" block: 125%
12" x 12" block: 150%

Directions for calculating the percentage of enlargement or reduction for other block sizes appear on page 7.

The Breton Fisherman's Knot fills the same amount of space whether the block is set straight or on point.

The Welsh Tulip can fit into a smaller block when the block is set on point.

Breton Fisherman's Knot

CELTIC DECORATIVE STYLE is found not only in the British Isles but also in the French province of Brittany, where carved wooden chests from the sixteenth and seventeenth centuries display Celtic designs of stunning quality. These designs—this knot pattern among them—are easy to adapt for quilting. Many of these patterns were recorded by Charles Le Roux and published in *Ornamentation Bretonne*.

Breton Fisherman's Knot
Variation A

A simple line filling gives the loops a
leaflike appearance in this reoriented
version (rotated 30°).

Breton Fisherman's Knot
Variation B

Filling the in-between spaces with
parallel lines raises the loops' profile
on the quilt surface.

Placement Guide

Knotted Circle

ORIGINALLY DESCRIBED as a "knot with three loops," this Celtic-style pattern is reminiscent of sailors' rope work. Its simple, interlacing form can be stitched by hand or machine.

Knotted Circle
Variation A

*Double lining and cross-hatching gives a
geometry to the spaces inside the loops.*

Knotted Circle
Variation B

*This reoriented version (rotated 30°)
is contained within an outer double
circle and echo-filled.*

Placement Guide

Weardale Wheel

THIS CLASSIC PATTERN from the dales (valleys) of Northern England is named after the huge waterwheel in Weardale, which powered early lead mining there. Some of England's best nineteenth-century quilts and quilting patterns came from Weardale.

Weardale Wheel
Variation A

A simple double-lined adaptation emphasises the swirling nature of the pattern.

Weardale Wheel
Variation B

Filling with meander quilting or another filler raises the profile of the wheel spokes. Note that this variation is rotated 30°.

Placement Guide

Scalloped Circle

ORIGINALLY FROM A FRENCH WOOD CARVING, this particular pattern has many possible variations. Based on circles and segments of circles, the spaces inside can be used to transform the basic motif. Similar patterns can be drafted easily with a compass.

Scalloped Circle
Variation A

Echo filling the spaces around the circles and reorienting the pattern 45° produces an attractive cruciform variation.

Scalloped Circle
Variation B

Filling the outer semicircles with a random pattern raises the profile of the inner sections. Stipple quilting by hand or meander filling by machine are suitable choices.

Placement Guide

Shell

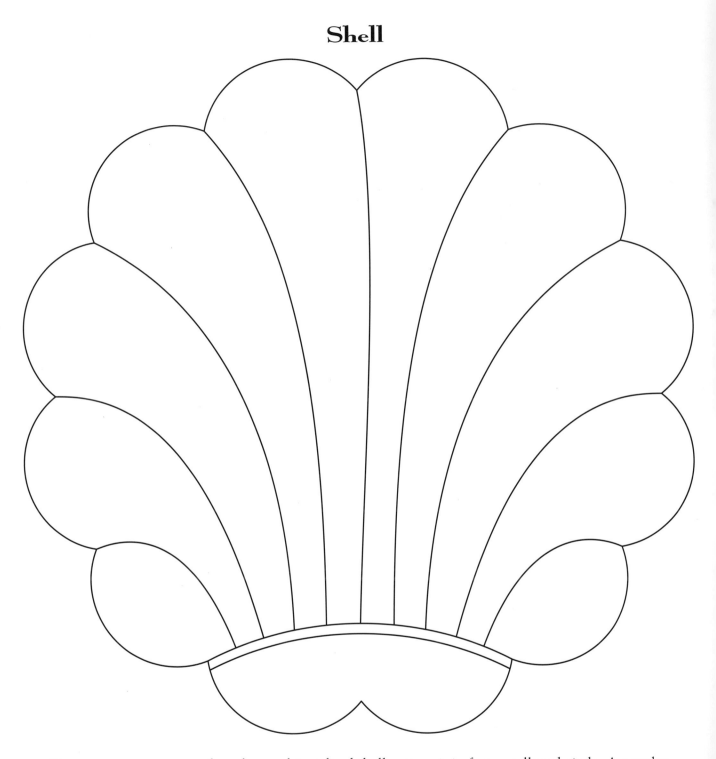

THOUGH NOT APPARENT at first glance, this stylised shell pattern is in fact a scalloped circle. A popular motif in many cultures, this particular version comes from the English North Country. It was especially popular on early-twentieth-century whole-cloth quilts.

Shell
Variation A

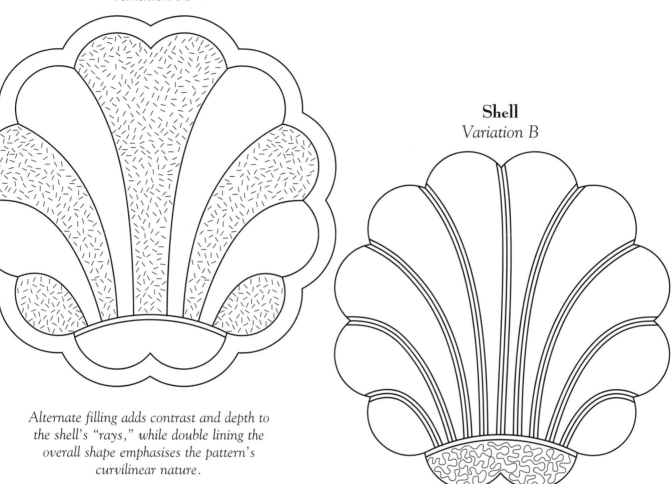

Shell
Variation B

Alternate filling adds contrast and depth to the shell's "rays," while double lining the overall shape emphasises the pattern's curvilinear nature.

Close quilting lines marking the "rays" accentuate the shell structure of the pattern.

Placement Guide

Faceted Circle

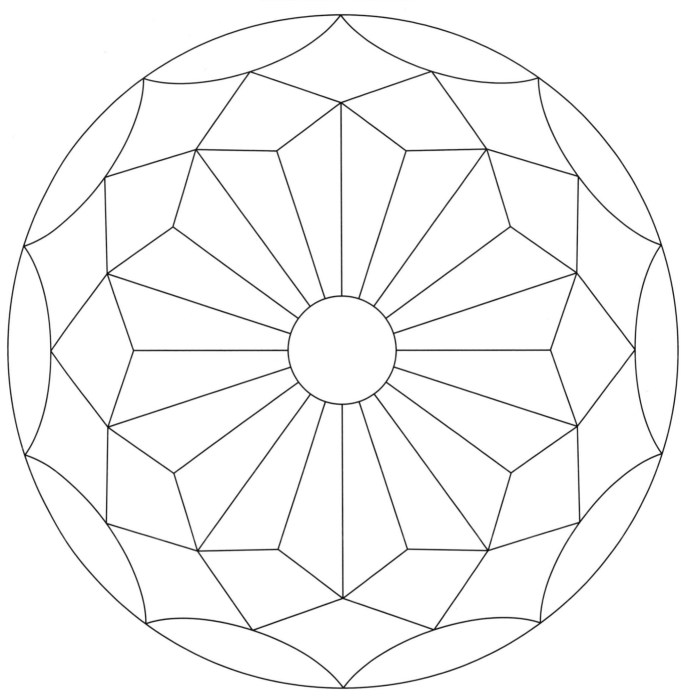

A COMBINATION OF straight and curved lines divide this pattern, based on a thirteenth-century rose window in the cathedral in Chartres, France. Its many internal divisions work best on a large scale. Doubled in size, the pattern is ideal for a quilted pillow.

 *Enlarge full-scale pattern by:*

125% to fit into a 10" x 10" block
150% to fit into a 12" x 12" block
200% to fit into a 16" x 16" block

Faceted Circle
Variation A

Graphic interest and a three-dimensional quality are created by alternately filling the facets with a random pattern. Note that this variation is rotated 18° because the pattern has a tenfold symmetry.

Faceted Circle
Variation B

This Star within a Circle variation gives the pattern internal depth.

Placement Guide

Looped Circle

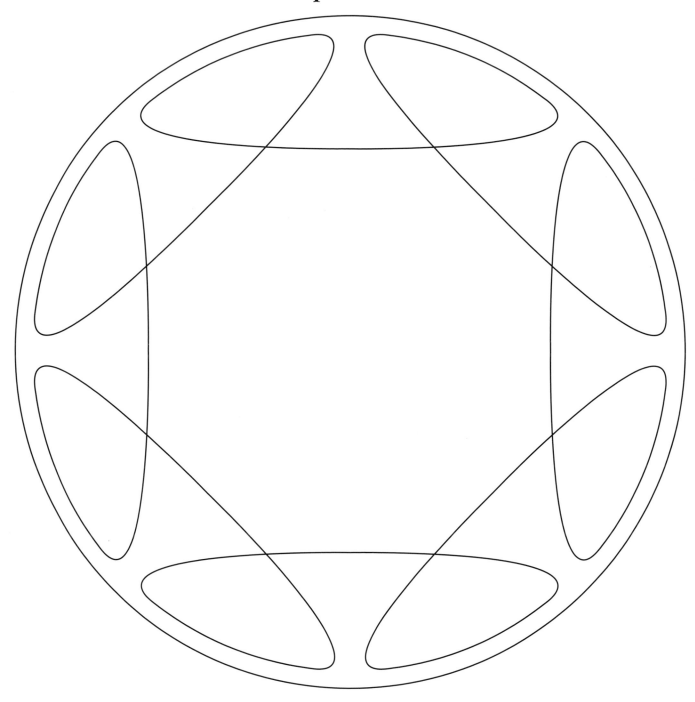

AN ORIGINAL DESIGN developed with computer software, this circle is ideal for machine quilting because the interior line is continuous.

Looped Circle
Variation A

With the addition of a few lines and small "eyes" of close filler quilting, the pattern is transformed into the illusion of a central square on point. Rotate 45° and the central shape will be set straight.

Looped Circle
Variation B

Another simple variation, combining curved and straight lines, this pattern can also be rotated 22½°.

Placement Guide

Abertridwr Star

IN SOUTH WALES in the 1930s, young quilters were formally taught to produce quilts for sale in London galleries. They were also encouraged to develop new motifs. This original star design was created by Katy Lewis of Abertridwr and named after her village.

Abertridwr Star
Variation A

Dropping internal lines and triple lining the outline of the motif raises the profile of the star's internal sections.

Abertridwr Star
Variation B

This simpler, reoriented variation (with fewer internal lines) nevertheless retains the fluid quality of the original.

Placement Guide

Star in a Square

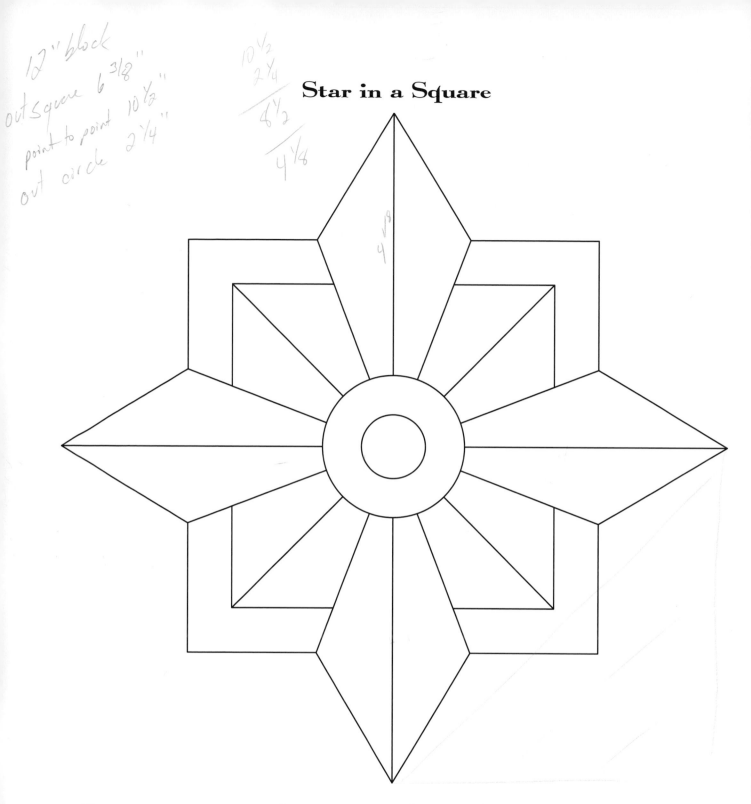

TAKEN FROM A TWELFTH-CENTURY FRENCH MANUSCRIPT, this pattern has a bold geometry, making it ideal for quilting. It is equally effective set on point and will fit into a smaller block with this orientation. (See below.) *Full-scale pattern will fit into an 8" x 8" block set straight or a 7" x 7" block set on point.*

Enlarge/reduce full-scale pattern by:

75% to fit into a 6" x 6" block set straight or a 5½" x 5½" block set on point
125% to fit into a 10" x 10" block set straight or a 9" x 9" block set on point
150% to fit into a 12" x 12" block set straight or a 10½" x 10½" block set on point

28

Star in a Square
Variation A

Filling the inner square and inner circle adds contrast and depth to the pattern.

Square in a Square
Variation B

Adding and subtracting a few lines and turning the square on point creates a simple but pleasing variation.

Placement Guide

Compass Star

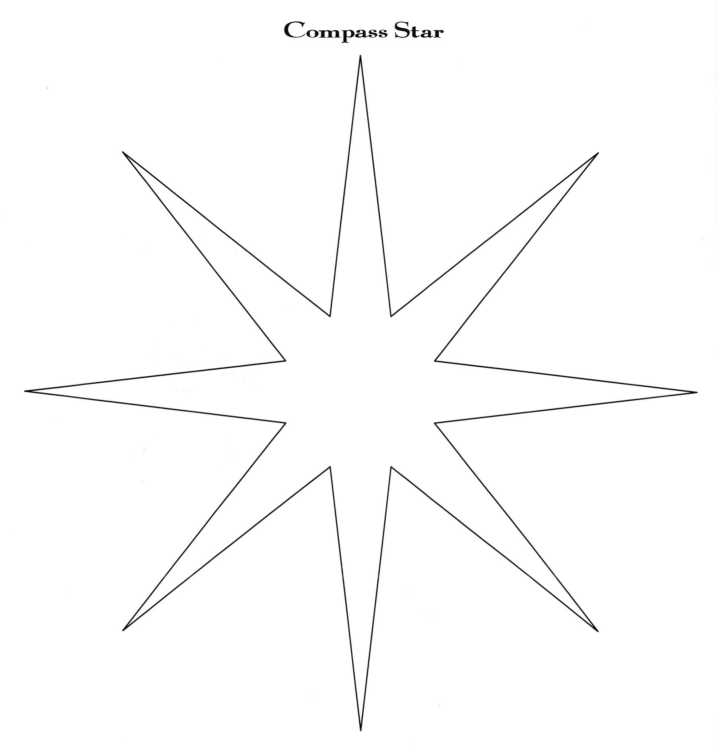

MARINER'S COMPASS has long been popular as a pieced pattern, but it can be effective as a quilting pattern too. The sharply angular compass points of this Eight-Pointed Star define a simple but graphic outline. *Full-scale pattern will fit into a 7½" x 7½" block set straight or on point.*

 *Enlarge/reduce full-scale pattern by:*

80% to fit into a 6" x 6" block
125% to fit into a 9½" x 9½" block
150% to fit into an 11½" x 11½" block

Compass Star
Variation A

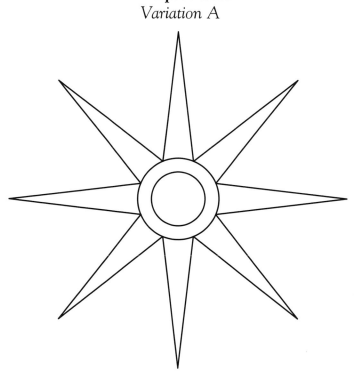

Two concentric inner circles bring a stronger focus to the pattern; they can be filled or left unfilled as shown here.

Compass Star
Variation B

The internal **V***s created by connecting the points are alternately filled with a dense filler pattern. To retain a symmetrical look, rotate the pattern 22½° as shown.*

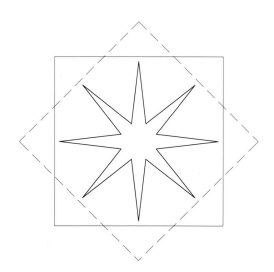

Placement Guide

Star of Diamonds

THE STRONG GEOMETRY of this original design, based on diamonds and a hexagon, creates a bold, six-pointed star. Particularly suitable for machine quilting, it can be used either as an individual pattern or in pattern groups. (See page 10.) It is equally effective rotated 30°.

Star of Diamonds
Variation A

Star of Diamonds
Variation B

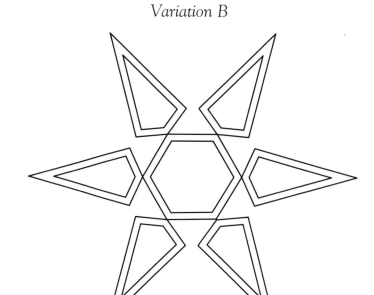

Double lining the outside edge, then filling the space around the hexagon and diamond shapes creates a larger pattern with depth and contrast.

Simple double lining emphasises the bold geometry of this version (rotated 30°).

Placement Guide

FEATHERS, FANS, AND FERNS

Princess Feather

Connect to bottom half, page 35.

PERHAPS BETTER KNOWN as an American appliqué pattern, the Princess Feather is also a large and dramatic quilting pattern. Seldom used as an isolated motif, it is best combined for quilt centres.

Connect to top half, page 34.

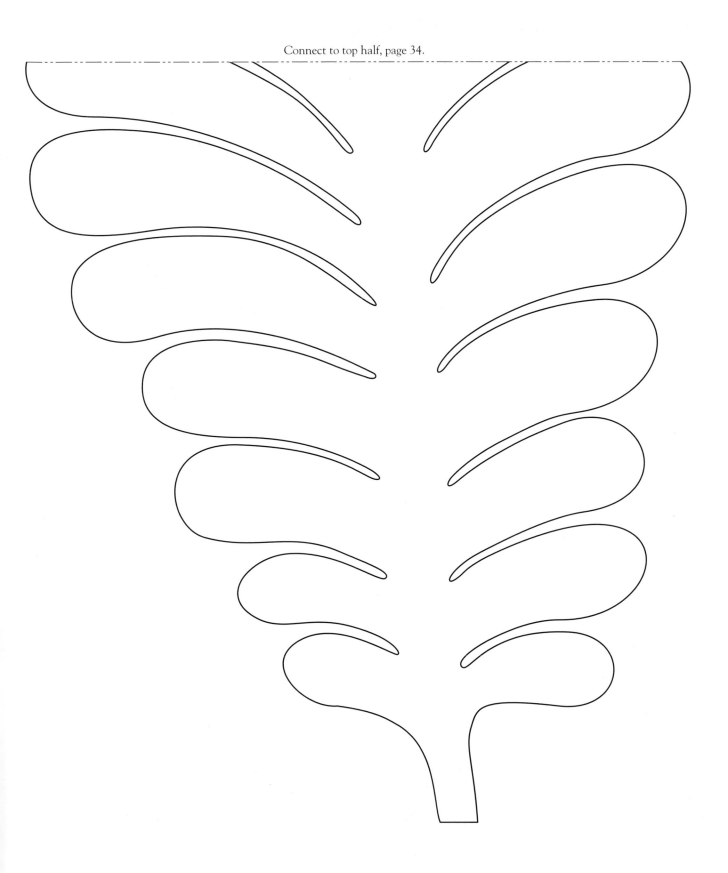

Princess Feather

An eightfold circular group of feathers is the classic way of using this pattern.
Rotate the motifs 22½° for a different orientation. Eight full-scale
patterns will fit around an 8"-diameter circular space to
create a centre design approximately 40" in diameter.

Curled Feather

Connect to bottom half, page 38.

A SWIRL OF FEATHERS is one of the hallmarks of English North Country quilting, but feather patterns have a long history in quilting around the world, dating back at least to the eighteenth century. This English North Country pattern is a twentieth-century version, but its elegant form is equal to that of earlier patterns.

Connect to top half, page 37.

Curled Feather
Group A

*Three feathers, a mirror-image pair and a third
in the centre, fill a corner in flowing style.
Full-scale patterns will fit into a corner
space 16" x 16".*

 *arge/reduce full-scale pattern by:*

75% to fit into a corner space 12" x 12"
125% to fit into a corner space 20" x 20"

Curled Feather
Group B

An eightfold arrangement of curled feathers set in mirror-image pairs around a circular space makes a dramatic quilt centre. Eight full-scale patterns will fit around a 6½"-diameter circular space to create a centre design approximately 32" in diameter.

Feather Wreath

ONE OF THE MOST POPULAR QUILTING PATTERNS around the world, this versatile wreath can be used for quilt centres, in setting blocks, or enlarged for a pillow design. Wherever this pattern appears, its fluid movement draws the eye into the design. It needs little variation and combines well with other patterns.

Full-scale pattern will fit into an 8" x 8" block set straight or on point.

 *Enlarge full-scale pattern by:*

150% to fit into a 12" x 12" block
200% to fit into a 16" x 16" block

Feather Wreath
Variation A

*A simple outer double line sharpens
the pattern outline.*

Feather Wreath
Variation B

*Encircling the pattern, then filling the outer
and inner spaces with stipple quilting raises
the profile of the feather plumes. Don't forget
to allow more space for this variation.*

Placement Guide

Penny Ha'penny

SOMETIMES KNOWN AS Feather Swag, the "Penny Ha'penny" name used by Amy Emms—that most famous of Durham quilters—has much more traditional resonance. It comes from the original method of using old English pennies and halfpennies to mark the scallop outlines of the feather. Seldom used as an isolated pattern, it can be combined for borders, quilt centres, or setting blocks.

Penny Ha'penny
Group A

This fourfold plan makes an attractive quilt centre or design for a large setting block. Four full-scale patterns will fit as drawn into an 18" x 18" space or block set straight, or a 15½" x 15½" block set on point.

Enlarge full-scale pattern by:

125% to fit into a 22½" x 22½" space or block set straight, or a 20" x 20" block set on point

Penny Ha'penny
Group B

Used in an eightfold plan, Penny Ha'penny
creates a scalloped circle outline
for a quilt centre.
Eight full-scale patterns as drawn will create
a circular design 26" in diameter.

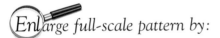 Enlarge full-scale pattern by:

125% to create a centre design
32½" in diameter

Penny Ha'penny
Group C

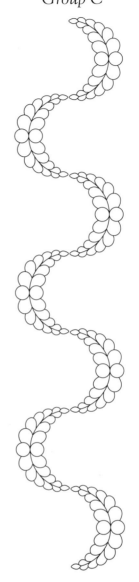

A chain of patterns, with every other one
flipped over, makes a fluid border design.
Use an odd number for a
symmetrical arrangement.
Seven evenly spaced full-scale patterns
will fit as drawn into a border 10" x 50".

 Enlarge full-scale pattern by:

125% to fit a border 12½" x 62½"
150% to fit a border 15" x 75"

Goosewing

VARIOUS FORMS OF THE GOOSEWING PATTERN have come from the English North Country. All are basically a feather motif with "plumes" on only one side. Used in pairs, this motif makes elegant border and centre designs.

44

Goosewing
Group A

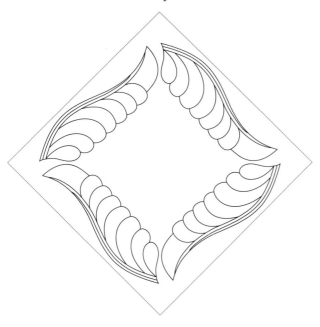

This fourfold arrangement with the plumes
facing toward the centre brings movement
to the outer edge, but leaves a nice
scalloped internal space.
Four full-scale patterns will fit as drawn
into a 12½" x 12½" block or space.

*Enl*arge full-scale pattern by:

125% to fit into a 16" x 16" block or space
150% to fit into a 19" x 19" block or space

Goosewing
Group B

This border grouping uses pairs
of Goosewings set at 45°
across the border.
The plumed sides face the same
direction within the border.
Eight evenly spaced full-scale
patterns will fit as drawn into
an 8" x 70" border.

*Enl*arge full-scale pattern by:

125% to fit a 10" x 87½" border

Goosewing
Group C

Though similar to Group B,
here every other Goosewing is a
mirror-image pattern. This produces
a curving border with one smooth
edge and one scalloped edge.
Eight evenly spaced full-scale patterns
will fit as drawn into an 8" x 70" border.

*Enl*arge full-scale pattern by:

125% to fit a 10" x 87½" border

Fan

THIS SIMPLE FAN DESIGN IS another versatile pattern. Basically a quartered scalloped circle, it can be used either on its own as a corner pattern or in combination for blocks and borders.

Fan
Group A

Setting a Fan in each corner of a block
creates an attractive scalloped centre space.
(See page 6 for a sixfold setting of Fans.)
Four full-scale patterns will fit as drawn
into the corners of a 15" x 15" block. Rotate
the block 45° to set it on point.

Enlarge/reduce full-scale pattern by:

75% to fit into an 11½" x 11½" block
125% to fit into a 19" x 19" block

Fan
Group B

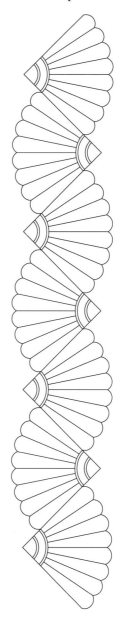

Setting Fans in a line with every other one
reversed creates a sinuous border design
popular among early-twentieth-century
North Country quilters.
Seven evenly spaced full-scale patterns will
fit as drawn into a 9" x 48" border.

Enlarge full-scale pattern by:

125% to fit a 11½" x 60" border
150% to fit a 13½" x 72" border

Peacock Fan

ESSENTIALLY A SEMICIRCLE, the stylised American Peacock Fan pattern is simple and leaflike. It would not look out of place combined with flower and leaf patterns.

Peacock Fan

Set in a fourfold radial group, the motifs create an attractive curved centre space.
Four full-scale patterns will fit as drawn into a 17" x 17" block set
straight or an 15" x 15" block set on point.

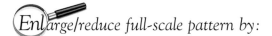 *Enlarge/reduce full-scale pattern by:*

75% to fit into a 13" x 13" block set straight or a 11½" x 11½" block set on point
125% to fit into a 21½" x 21½" block set straight or a 19" x 19" block set on point

Small Fern

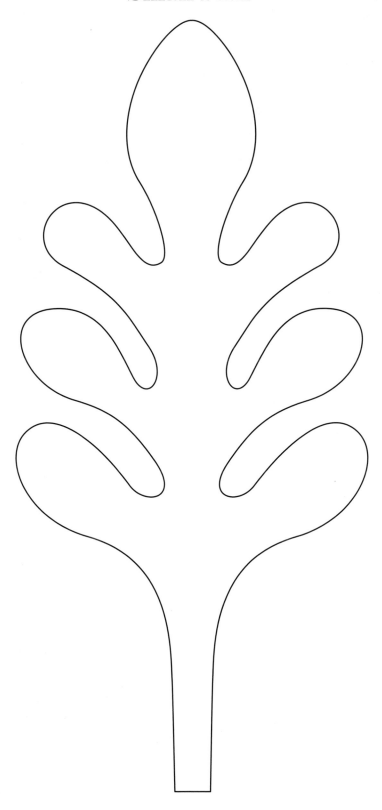

STRAIGHT AND SYMMETRICAL, Small Fern is similar in style to Small Leaf (page 52). Use it in combination for best effect.

Small Fern
Group A

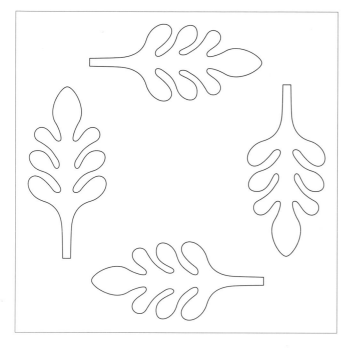

*A fourfold combination, set in a
clockwise rotation, fills a setting block.
Four full-scale patterns will fit as drawn
into a 15" x 15" block.*

Enlarge/reduce full-scale pattern by:

75% to fit into a 11½" x 11½" block
125% to fit into a 19" x 19" block

Small Fern
Group B

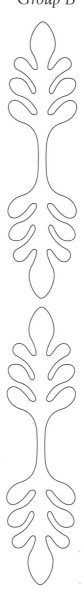

*Mirror-image pairs with overlapping
stems make an effective chain that
works well in sashing strips.
Full-scale patterns will fit into a 4½"-wide
border or strip set. Each pair requires 15"
in length (allowing for a 1" stem overlap).*

Small Leaf

WITH ITS SCALLOPED OUTLINE and curved internal lines, the Small Leaf pattern is typical of English North Country designs. Its formal, stylised outline makes it ideal as an individual pattern, but it is too static to attach to a stem or trailing vine.

Small Leaf
Variation A

*Close filler quilting raises the profile
of the central stem.*

Small Leaf
Variation B

*In contrast, close quilting along the
central stem depresses that area.*

Placement Guide

*Four full-scale patterns will fit as drawn into a 12" x 12"
block set straight or a 10" x 10" block set on point.*

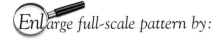 *Enlarge full-scale pattern by:*

150% to fit into an 18" x 18" block set
straight or a 15" x 15" block set on point
200% to fit into a 24" x 24" block set
straight or a 20" x 20" block set on point

Cardiganshire Corner Leaf

FROM RURAL WALES (Cardiganshire, now called Dyfed) comes this heart-shaped leaf customarily used in the corners of a quilt design.

Cardiganshire Corner Leaf
Variation A

Double lined and stitched with space-filling spirals, this variation maintains the essence of the Welsh style.

Cardiganshire Corner Leaf
Variation B

Close-filled "lenses" add depth and contrast within the pattern, but the spiral form keeps it Welsh.

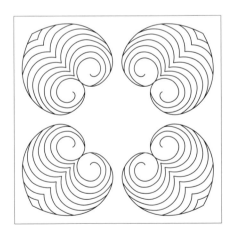

Placement Guide

*Closely set in the corners of a square, four repeats create an excellent pillow or block design.
Four full-scale patterns will fit as drawn into a 11" x 11" block.*

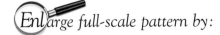 *Enlarge full-scale pattern by:*

150% to fit into a 16½" x 16½" block
200% to fit into a 22" x 22" block

Welsh Bent Leaf

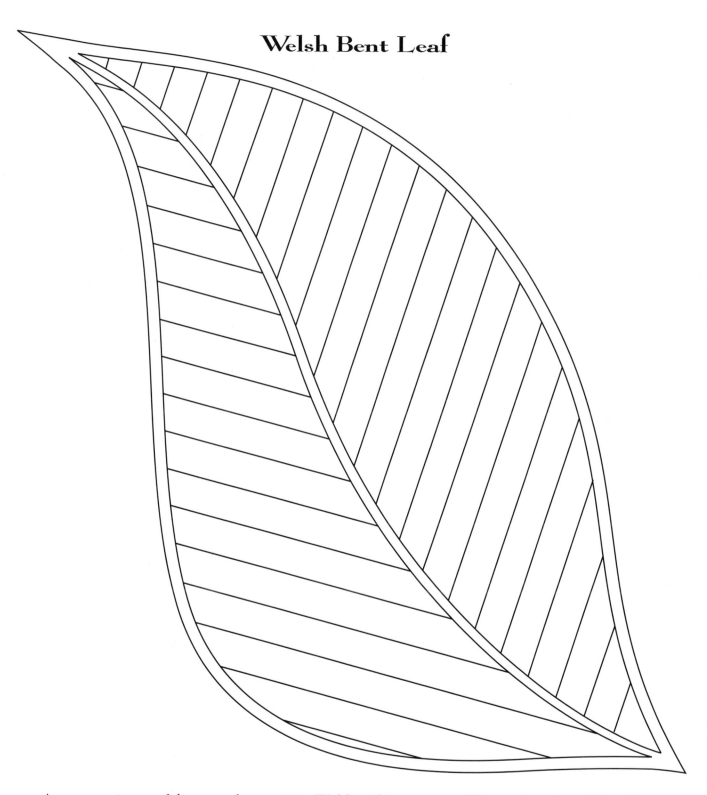

A BENT LEAF is one of the most characteristic Welsh quilting patterns. This version, though less elegant as an individual pattern, creates flowing, dynamic quilting designs when combined in a radial pattern for setting blocks or in mirror-image pairs for borders.

Welsh Bent Leaf
Variation A

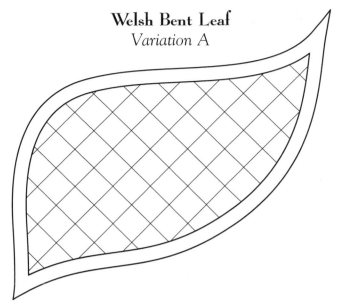

A simple crosshatched filling inside the double-lined pattern is a popular variation found on nineteenth-century Welsh quilts.

Welsh Bent Leaf
Variation B

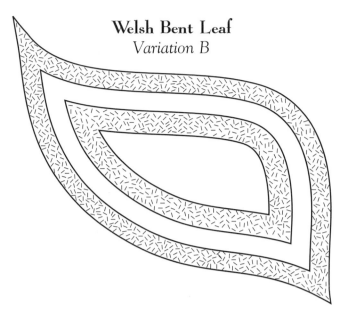

Filler quilting in alternate internal sections gives a more contemporary feel in a variation for hand or machine quilting.

Welsh Bent Leaf
Group A

Four full-scale patterns will fit as drawn into a 22" x 22" block set straight or a 16" x 16" block set on point.

Reduce full-scale pattern by:
75% to fit into a 16½" x 16½" block set straight or a 12" x 12" block set on point

Welsh Bent Leaf
Group B

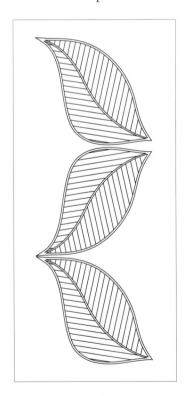

Mirror-image pairs of the full-scale pattern will fit as drawn across an 8"-wide border. Each pair needs 16" of border length.

Acanthus Leaf

FLUID AND ASYMMETRIC, the American Acanthus Leaf is a less formal pattern. Its deeply indented lobes and close lines make it particularly suitable for machine quilting, especially on a small scale.

Acanthus Leaf
Variations A and B

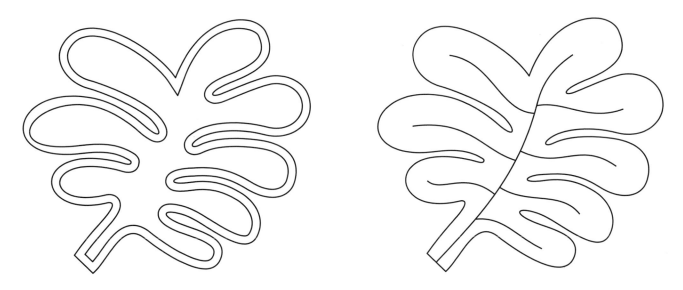

This pattern's deeply convoluted shape makes elaborate variations unnecessary.
Both double lining and simple veining retain the integrity of the pattern.

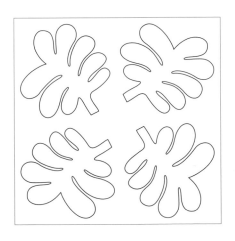

Placement Guide

Because of the asymmetric nature of the
pattern, a formally arranged radial group
is less appropriate than this looser block plan.
Four full-scale patterns will fit as drawn into
a 14" x 14" block set straight.

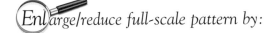 Enlarge/reduce full-scale pattern by:

75% to fit into a 10½" x 10½" block
125% to fit into a 17½" x 17½" block

Sunflower

THE BOLD, BRIGHT, AND BEAUTIFUL sunflower is an ever-popular folk-art motif. This quilted version comes from Northern England, where it figured prominently as the centrepiece of whole-cloth quilts, surrounded by a variety of leaf and flower motifs.

Sunflower
Variation A

Cross-hatching in the flower centre and filler in the space between the outer double lines create areas of depth and raise the profile of the petals.

Sunflower
Variation B

Changing the petal-base overlaps and echo filling the centre and background petals gives this simple variant a more cruciform look.

Placement Guide

North Country Tulip

THE TALL SHAPE OF THIS ENGLISH TULIP PATTERN contrasts with the squat Welsh form (page 64). Although static and formal as an individual pattern, the sinuous outline develops fluidity and movement when the pattern is repeated. A simple fourfold combination works well as a pillow design.

North Country Tulip
Variation A

Closing up the lines of the original pattern yields this double- and triple-lined version.

North Country Tulip
Variation B

Double lining the outer petals while cross-hatching the centre gives depth to the flower centre.

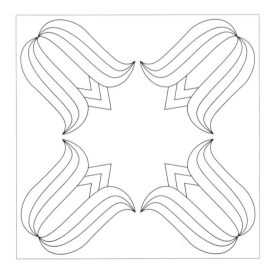

Placement Guide

Four full-scale patterns will fit as drawn into an 18" x 18" setting block or pillow square. Rotate the block 45° to set it on point.

Reduce full-scale pattern by: 67% to fit into a 12" x 12" block

Welsh Tulip

THIS WIDER, MORE OPEN TULIP comes from Wales. Although often used as a single corner motif, its sinuous curves create interesting spaces when the units are combined.

Welsh Tulip
Group A

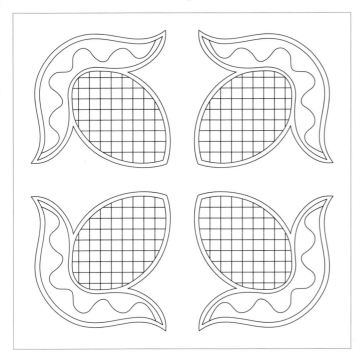

In the classic fourfold setting, the Welsh
Tulip forms a strong cruciform centre.
Boldly filled, the centre can become
the focus of the design.
Four full-scale patterns will fit as
drawn into a 13" x 13" block.

Enlarge *full-scale pattern by:*

125% to fit into a 16½" x 16½" block
150% to fit into a 19" x 19" block

Welsh Tulip
Group B

In a sixfold, outward-facing radial group,
Welsh Tulips form a curved star
in the centre.
Six full-scale patterns will fit as drawn
around an 8" circle. The arrangement
is approximately 20" in diameter
(point to point).

Enlarge/reduce *full-scale pattern by:*

75% to fit around a 6" circle
(15" overall diameter)
125% to fit around a 10" circle
(25" overall diameter)

Welsh Tulip
Variation A

Spiral fillers and a leaf-patterned centre
maintain the traditional Welsh
spirit of the pattern.

Welsh Tulip
Variation B

A close fill in the petals raises the profile of
the centre and gives the pattern a more
contemporary feel.

Snowdrop

SOMETIMES YOU NEED A SMALL PATTERN to link other motifs or to fill a small space. I developed this original pattern for the purpose of linking together quilted swags. Small patterns can also be linked in chains to act as separators on the quilt surface.

Snowdrop
Group A

Linked in a chain of sixteen with every other pattern flipped, the Snowdrop makes an ideal outer frame for a central pattern. Sixteen full-scale patterns will fit as drawn into a 15½" block or circular space.

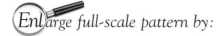 *arge full-scale pattern by:*

125% to fit into a 19½" block or space
150% to fit into a 24" block or space

Snowdrop
Variations A and B

Double lining, triple lining, and close filling create two simple Snowdrop options.

Rose in a Ring

QUILTERS IN THE NORTH OF ENGLAND were fond of rose patterns and created many variations on the scalloped-circle theme. Rose in a Ring was a popular twentieth-century version. It is an ideal quilt or pillow centrepiece and also makes a wonderful setting-block pattern.

Rose in a Ring
Variation A

*Close fill around the petals brings
them into relief.*

Rose in a Ring
Variation B

*Filling the petals of the outer rose brings the
inner rose into relief.*

Placement Guide

Miscellany

The patterns in this section are personal favourites with either particular associations, historical connections, very specific uses, or a strong, individual style. Like the other patterns in the book, they can be varied or combined in multiunits. They work particularly well as individual, "stand-alone" motifs.

Celtic Bell

THE INTERTWINING BELLS of this Celtic motif from France, recorded by Charles Le Roux in *Ornamentation Bretonne*, translate into a stunning quilting pattern. A combination of straight lines and curves, the pattern can be stitched by hand or machine. The square frame formed by the outer lines of the design makes this motif ideally suited to setting blocks and pillow tops.

Placement Guide

*Set straight, the full-scale pattern
will fit into an 8" x 8" block.*

 *arge full-scale pattern by:*

150% to fit into a 12" x 12" block
200% to fit into a 16" x 16" block

Placement Guide

*Rotated 45°, the full-scale pattern will
fit into an 11" x 11" block.*

 *arge full-scale pattern by:*

125% to fit into a 14" x 14" block
150% to fit into a 16½" x 16½" block

True Lover's Knot

THE TRUE LOVER'S KNOT is an ancient Celtic design. Its strands, like true love, have no apparent end. One of many "endless" or "magic" knot designs found in different folk cultures, this pattern was common on English North Country quilts in the late nineteenth and early twentieth centuries. It has also been found on Amish quilts. Contrary to popular belief, its presence does not necessarily indicate a wedding quilt.

Placement Guide

*Full-scale pattern will fit into an 8" x 8"
block set straight or on point.*

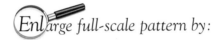 *arge full-scale pattern by:*

150% to fit into a 12" x 12" block
200% to fit into a 16" x 16" block

Mrs. Boundy's Tulip

LIKE KATY LEWIS (page 26), Mrs. Boundy was taught to quilt in South Wales in the 1930s. She developed a remarkably individual style and distinctive motifs, including this double-lined tulip with its cigar-shaped stem. When a whole-cloth quilt bearing this and other motifs closely linked with Mrs. Boundy was discovered in Australia fifty years later, it was possible to identify her as its probable maker.

Placement Guide

Full-scale pattern will fit into a 9" x 9" block set straight or on point.

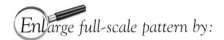 *Enlarge full-scale pattern by:*

125% to fit into an 11½" x 11½" block
150% to fit into a 13½" x 13½" block

French Swirl

THIS STYLISH MOTIF comes from a seventeenth-century French ossuary. Although a pattern of some antiquity, it has a surprisingly contemporary feel. Its swirling movement and square form make it ideal for quilting. Set straight or on point, it can be used alone in setting blocks or combined in larger groups.

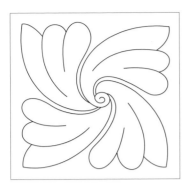

Placement Guide

*Full-scale pattern set straight will
fit into an 8" x 8" block.*

Enlarge/reduce full-scale pattern by:

75% to fit into a 6" x 6" block
125% to fit into a 10" x 10" block
150% to fit into a 12" x 12" block

Placement Guide

*Rotated 45°, full-scale pattern will fit
into an 11" x 11" block.*

Enlarge/reduce full-scale pattern by:

75% to fit into an 8½" x 8½" block
125% to fit into a 14" x 14" block
150% to fit into a 16½" x 16½" block

Eight-Point Centre

THESE SEEMINGLY UNSPECTACULAR PATTERNS fall into the indispensable category. As quilt centres, they have two distinct advantages: 1) quilted with the filler pattern of your choice, the centre space acts as a simple yet dramatic focal point; and 2) the outer points give precise positions for patterns surrounding the centre. (See Group C on pages 86–87.)

Six-Point Centre

Welsh Spiral

TIGHTLY COILED SPIRALS, large and small, are the most common motif on Welsh quilts. An ancient design, the spiral appears in prehistoric stone carvings, where its real significance can only be guessed at. As a quilting pattern, it was used in formally arranged groups or chains or as an individual motif with spirals up to 12" in diameter.

Placement Guide

Pattern Groups

In looking at old quilts—especially whole-cloth quilts—I quickly discovered that some of the best ones used a variety of patterns. I often found that the larger the variety, the better the design.

Some designs looked very elaborate and ornate. Closer investigation revealed that they were not necessarily difficult to plan. Most pattern combinations on traditional quilts rely on the radial group principle—combining patterns in a fourfold, sixfold, or eightfold symmetry.

To help you plan and precisely mark pattern combinations, three examples have been set out here. These pattern combinations have been reduced to fit the page, but the space each pattern group will fit is given.

If you feel nervous about marking a design directly onto fabric, try drafting the full-scale pattern combination onto paper first, then trace the paper design onto fabric as you would an individual pattern. (Complete directions for marking quilting designs begin on page 88.)

Group A. Centre Design
with Eightfold Symmetry

Small Leaf (page 52)

Rose in a Ring (page 68)

This group measures 19" in diameter.

1. Find the centre of the fabric (or paper) by folding it into quarters and marking the centre with a removable mark or pin.

2. Crease lightly (or baste) along the folds.

3. Using the full-scale Rose in a Ring pattern (page 68) or a stencil made from it, match the centre of the fabric (or paper) and the centre of the pattern. Make sure the pattern is correctly oriented on the fabric (see diagram).

4. Carefully trace or mark the pattern, then add a double line approximately ¼" from the pattern outline as shown.

5. Using the Small Leaf pattern (page 52) or a stencil made from it, mark 8 leaves at 45° intervals around the Rose in a Ring. Set each pattern ½" from the double line around the Rose in a Ring, measuring from the valley of the scallop. Begin by marking the leaves at the top, bottom, and sides, placing them along the folds (or basting). The centre of each stem and the tip of each leaf should line up exactly along the crease.

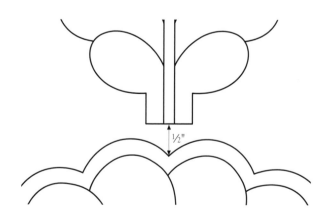

6. Mark the remaining 4 leaf patterns, using the 45° line on your quilters' ruler. Align the 45° mark on the ruler with the centre of one of the previously drawn leaves. The ruler's edge should be aligned with the centre line of the adjacent leaf.

7. Finally, draw a double line ¼" outside the leaves, drawing around the point and top two lobes of each leaf, then joining the lines between each leaf as shown in the diagram on the previous page.

Group B. Centre Design
with Sixfold Symmetry

Knotted Circle (page 14)

Cardiganshire Corner Leaf (page 54)

This group measures 17½" in diameter.

1. Find the centre of the fabric (or paper) to be marked by folding it in quarters and marking the centre with a removable mark or pin.
2. Crease lightly (or baste) along the vertical fold.
3. Using the Knotted Circle pattern (page 14) or a stencil made from it, locate the centre of the pattern by drawing lines across the points of the "hexagon" in the centre. The centre of the pattern is where the lines cross.
4. Match the centre of the pattern with the centre of the fabric (or paper), and align one of the drawn lines on the pattern with the vertical crease (or basting) on the fabric.
5. Carefully mark the Knotted Circle pattern.
6. Using the Cardiganshire Corner Leaf pattern (page 54), mark 6 patterns at 60° intervals. Set each pattern so the closest gap between each leaf and the Knotted Circle is ¼". Begin by marking the patterns at the top and bottom, making sure the centre and tip of each leaf lie along the fold (or basting).

7. Mark the leaf to the right of the top leaf by aligning the 60° angle on your quilters' ruler with the centre of the top leaf. Centre the next leaf along the edge of the ruler as described in step 6 on page 83. Mark the leaf, then reverse the process for the leaf on the left.
8. Mark the 2 remaining leaves in a similar fashion, using the bottom leaf as your guide. There should be about a ½" gap between leaves.
9. Using a tool for drawing circles, draw a 17" diameter circle around the pattern group. Draw another circle ¼" outside the first (17½" diameter).

Group C. Centre Design with Fourfold Symmetry

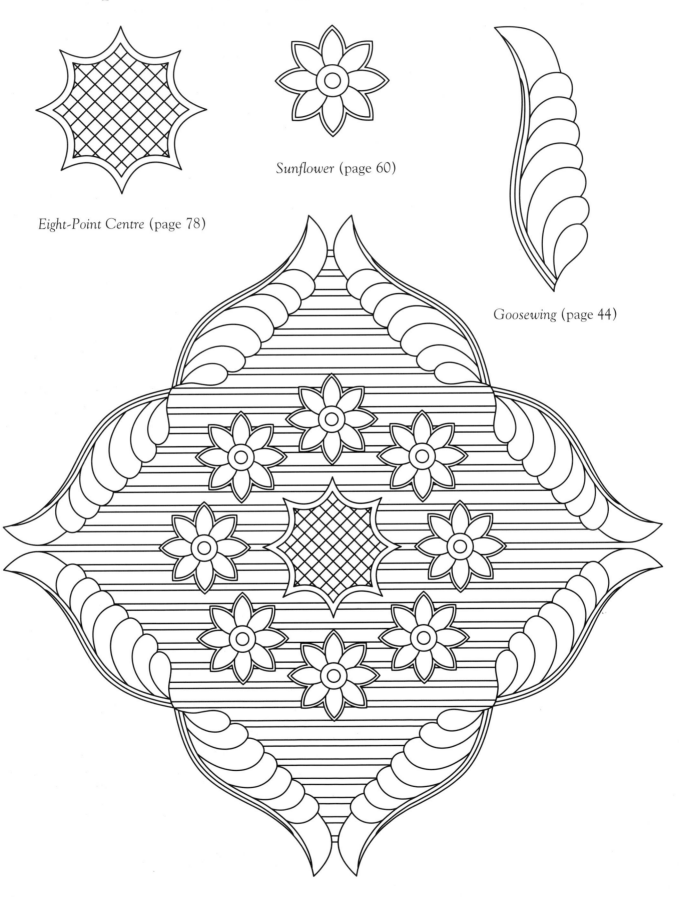

Eight-Point Centre (page 78)

Sunflower (page 60)

Goosewing (page 44)

This group measures 51" from corner to corner.

1. Find the centre of the fabric (or paper) to be marked by folding it in quarters and marking the centre with a removable mark or pin.

2. Crease lightly (or baste) along the folds.

3. Enlarge the Eight-Point Centre pattern (page 78) by 150%. Make a stencil if desired. Find the centre of the pattern or stencil (where the central cross-hatched lines intersect).

4. Matching the centre of the fabric (or paper) with the centre of the pattern, carefully mark the Eight-Point Centre.

5. Using the Sunflower pattern (page 60), mark 8 patterns at 45° intervals around the Eight-Point Centre. To correctly position the flowers, line up each point on the Eight-Point Centre with a sunflower as shown.

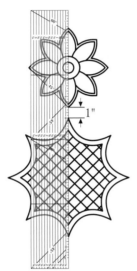

6. Enlarge the Goosewing pattern (page 44) by 175% and also make a mirror image of this enlargement. Now make templates (either outline or stencil templates, pages 89–90) for *both* patterns in this mirror-image pair—it is much easier to position the patterns in pairs on top of the fabric. Any slight adjustments can be made by shifting the templates on the fabric. With outline templates, you will need to trace the internal lines after the outlines are drawn.

7. Mark the 8 Goosewings that frame the centre design in 4 mirror-image pairs. Use 2 long rulers to help you position them correctly. Centre one end of each ruler on the design as shown. Lay the rulers out at a 45° angle to the folds, each one passing through a point on the Eight-Point Centre and 2 opposing petal points on the adjacent sunflower. Place the inner curves of the Goosewing tips close to the fold (or basting) as shown, and the Goosewing bases adjacent to the ruler edges. The tips should be approximately 12" from the point of the nearest sunflower petal, and the bases 4" away as indicated on the diagram below.

8. Fill the inner space around the drawn motifs with a filler pattern of double horizontal lines at 1½" intervals, beginning with double lines across the centre of the design.

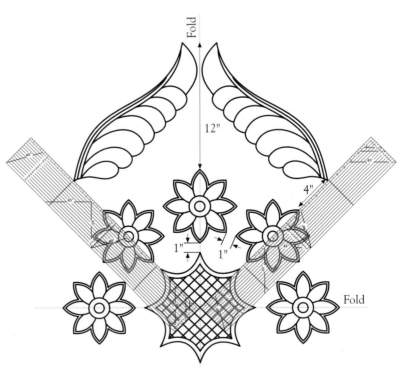

Note: Distances are approximate and slight adjustments
may be needed to maintain pattern symmetry.

Quilting Supplies and Techniques

MARKING

Before any piece of work can be quilted, the full quilting design needs to be marked on the fabric surface. The one exception is machine quilting through paper. (See page 93.) Ideally, the patterns need to be drawn with a fine line that is clearly visible when stitching, but either invisible or easy to remove when quilting is complete. Sounds simple! In practice, more discussion takes place over markers and marking methods than almost any other aspect of quilting.

Marking Tools

Despite the bewildering array of markers available, no single marker works for every fabric. Markers that show clearly on light-coloured fabrics are unsuitable for dark colours; ones for shiny fabrics do not work on matte surfaces. You may also need different markers depending on the techniques you choose. Some markers brush away easily, which makes them inappropriate for hoop quilting. And not everyone's eyes are the same—you are the best judge of what is clear to you.

With this in mind, choose from the following tools, presented in order of personal preference:

Lead pencil: Very useful for light (especially white) fabrics. Choose a mechanical pencil with a fine lead. A 0.5 mm lead is best, either H or HB. If the patterns are marked very lightly, the lines should not show when stitching is complete. Heavy lines may not wash out easily and may be visible on the finished quilt.

Silver or soapstone pencils: Useful for dark fabrics. Keep well sharpened and beware of lines fading if you spread your quilting over a period of time. Remove if necessary by washing.

Soap slivers: Also useful for dark fabrics. Wash out easily!

Pressure markers: Includes blunt needles, sharp-edged tools, and (less effective) tracing wheels. Useful for shiny fabrics and some delicate fabrics like silk. Completely invisible when quilting is complete, which is a great advantage. Can disappear quickly, depending on the fabric.

Dressmakers' coloured pencils: Useful if quilting in a frame, but marks can disappear with too much handling. Need to be kept sharp, but they break easily. Brush away or wash out.

Powdered chalk wheels: Available in different colours for light or dark fabrics, they leave an excellent fine line that disappears too easily with handling. Useful for re-marking any faint or faded lines on a work in progress.

Coloured pencils: Useful on strongly coloured fabrics. Choose a colour slightly darker than the fabric and keep it well sharpened. It should not show when quilting is complete.

Chalk: Easy to see on most surfaces and easy to remove by brushing, but leaves a very thick line. Not suitable for quilting in a hoop.

Water-soluble marker: Very useful for machine quilting when a bolder line is required. Needs to be washed out thoroughly in cold water, not just sponged away as often recommended. Lines will set with heat, so do not iron after marking. Potential long-term fabric damage, so only use on items not destined to be family heirlooms!

Always, always try a test sample first, using your chosen fabrics and batting. Mark a small pattern on a test square (say 10" x 10"), layer with batting and backing, quilt, then wash if the marks still show. If you encounter any problems seeing or removing the marks, try a different marker.

Marking Methods

Marking is a crucial stage in quilting; however carefully you stitch, if the patterns are badly drawn, the work will be flawed. Think carefully about which marker and which method to use.

Tracing

The patterns in this book are drawn for ease of tracing, and this is the preferred method of marking. There are four ways to trace patterns.

✤ *Light box.* Tape the pattern to a light box with masking tape. Place the fabric on top and secure. With the light turned on, the pattern shows clearly for tracing.

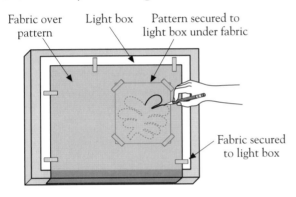

Fabric over pattern   Light box   Pattern secured to light box under fabric

Fabric secured to light box

✤ *Glass-topped table with a light source underneath.* Use the same way you would a light box.
✤ *Window.* Small items like pillow tops can be marked at a window. Tape the pattern to the window with masking tape, then position the fabric over the pattern and tape it to the window. Trace carefully, resting when your arms ache too much.
✤ *Tabletop.* Patterns with dark lines will show through most light fabrics on a tabletop. Tape the pattern to the table (not your best dining table) with masking tape, then secure the fabric on top and trace.

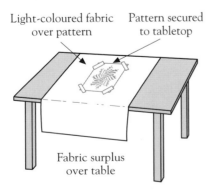

Light-coloured fabric over pattern   Pattern secured to tabletop

Fabric surplus over table

Outline Templates

An outline template produces the pattern outline without any of the internal lines. You lay it on the right side of your fabric and draw around it with your marking tool. Until the advent of light boxes and plastic templates, all quilting patterns were drawn onto fabric this way, with the internal lines drafted freehand. I still recommend this method for drawing naturalistic patterns, which look best when there are slight variations.

Outline templates can also be useful when multiples of the same pattern are used in a group. The precise position of each pattern can be marked with an outline template or set of outline templates, then the internal lines traced from a complete pattern or drawn in using a stencil. (The Goosewing motifs in Group C on page 87 were marked this way.) Choose either plastic or cardboard.

TO MAKE AN OUTLINE TEMPLATE:
✤ To make an outline template from template plastic, trace the pattern outline onto template plastic using a permanent marker. Cut out carefully.
✤ To make an outline template from cardboard, photocopy the pattern and glue it to thick cardboard. Cut out carefully on a cutting mat using scissors, a craft knife, or a scalpel.

TO MARK A PATTERN USING AN OUTLINE TEMPLATE:
1. Position template on the right side of fabric.
2. Holding template firmly in place, draw around it.
3. Draw the internal lines freehand, using the full pattern as a guide.

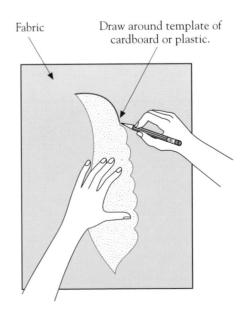

Fabric   Draw around template of cardboard or plastic.

Stencils

Stencils replicate all pattern lines, including internal lines, so the complete pattern can be marked from the top. They can be made from either plastic or cardboard.

Making your own stencils takes time, but for patterns that you want to use often, it may be worth the effort. Marking with stencils is straightforward, so long as you hold the stencil firmly on top of the fabric or secure it with tape.

To make a stencil:

1. Place a sheet of template plastic over the pattern. Trace the lines carefully with a permanent marker. Alternatively, photocopy the pattern and glue it to thick cardboard.
2. Using a craft knife or X-Acto™ knife and cutting mat, cut out a narrow space along the lines of the pattern about the width of the tip of your marking tool. Remember to leave a "bridge" every 1½" or so to keep the stencil intact.

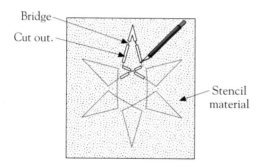

Bridge
Cut out.
Stencil material

To mark a pattern using a stencil:

1. Make sure your chosen marker will fit the space you cut out.
2. Secure the template in position with tape on the right side of the fabric and mark all pattern lines.

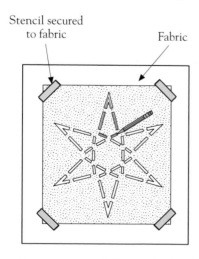

Stencil secured to fabric
Fabric

3. Remove the stencil and fill in the bridges.

BATTING

Like selecting markers, choosing batting generates much discussion and many questions. What's the best batting for hand quilting? Which battings drape best for bed quilts? What should be used for a small wall hanging that needs to keep its shape?

The choice is wide and getting wider all the time as new brands, fibre mixtures, and weights descend on the market. Trade regulations restrict the choice in some places; for example, some battings cannot be sold in certain countries because of fire regulations.

Battings come in natural fibres (cotton, silk, and wool) and synthetic (polyester), each with its own unique properties. Cotton and wool are also mixed with polyester to produce battings that, in theory, have the advantages of both fibres.

If you are in doubt about which batting to choose, ask a retailer for advice—they are usually up-to-date on new types and how good (or bad) they are. To simplify the choice, the chart below lists the common types of batting and their properties, both good and not-so-good.

Polyester
Inexpensive and widely available, by the yard and packaged, in a variety of weights and densities.

Dense forms are good for machine quilting and wall hangings because they do not shift.

Thinner varieties can stretch.

Harsh to handle and does not always drape well.

Cotton and Cotton/Polyester
Softer and better draping than 100% polyester. Retains loft better than polyester.

Dense forms are excellent for machine quilting and wall hangings.

Some brands shrink for an antique look.

Some 100%-cotton varieties can be difficult to hand quilt.

Wool and Wool/Polyester
Very soft, lightweight, and warm.

Expensive and not widely available.

Silk

Soft, luxurious, and a pleasure to handle and hand quilt.

Very expensive and not easily obtainable.

BASTING

Any quilted item is a sandwich of three layers: the quilt top, backing, and batting. To prevent these layers from shifting while you quilt (which can cause puckering or pleating), they are usually layered and basted together.

Basting is not always necessary when quilting in a full-size quilt frame. If you plan to machine or hand quilt using a hoop, however, careful layering and basting are essential.

TO BASTE A QUILT:

1. Cut the backing fabric and batting slightly larger than the quilt top (2" all around), unless you plan to use the backing fabric as a binding, in which case it will need to be even larger.
2. Iron the backing fabric, then lightly fold it into quarters and mark the centre and the midpoints of all edges with long, easily visible pins, such as flower-headed pins.

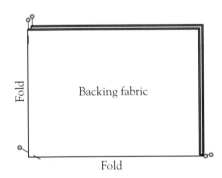

3. Open out the backing and place it right side down on a hard surface such as a tabletop or floor. Smooth out and secure with masking tape or clips.

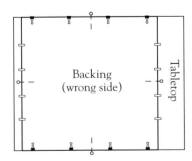

4. Fold the batting in quarters and mark the centre and the midpoints of all edges. Do not unfold. Lay the batting on one quarter of the backing, matching centres and placing the folds at the midpoints as shown. Unfold the batting once and smooth out, aligning the remaining fold at the midpoint as shown. Unfold the batting completely, matching the last midpoints. Secure lightly with tape or clips.

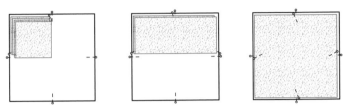

Unfold batting quadrant by quadrant, matching midpoints.

5. Iron the quilt top if necessary, then fold lightly in quarters, right side in. Repeat step 4, placing the quilt top right side up on the batting. Do not disturb the backing and batting. Secure with masking tape or pin through all three layers at the corners.

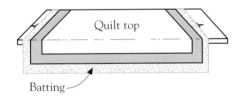

6. Baste the layers together, beginning in the centre and working outward, using one of the following methods:
   - Pin basting is generally used for machine quilting because hand-basting threads can get caught on parts of the machine. Use safety pins at approximately 4" intervals, but be wary of pin marks on delicate fabrics, especially for whole-cloth quilts. The finer flower-headed pins can be used in place of safety pins, but only for small items; be sure to push the sharp ends down into the fabric layers so you don't prick your fingers.
   - For thread basting, hand sew long stitches parallel to the quilt edges at intervals of 4" to 6". If thread basting for machine quilting, keep the stitches short (no more than ½") to prevent them from catching on the machine. Secure the ends of basting threads, since they can pop out.

Hand Quilting

Hand quilting produces a rhythm of stitches and spaces along the pattern lines. It is the broken nature of this quilted line that gives hand quilting its very special charm and character.

For hand quilting, choose quilting needles (Betweens) and quilting thread. Both are widely available. Contrasting, variegated, and metallic threads are popular and present a contemporary option to traditional white or matching thread.

For hoop quilting, begin in the centre of the quilt and work outwards. To quilt in a frame, begin at one end and work down the quilt, rolling the sections as you complete them. Do not leave knots or thread ends on the surface of the quilt. Begin each line of stitching by pulling the knotted end into the batting. End by backstitching or making a single French knot at the end and pulling it into the batting before cutting the thread.

Aim for neat, even stitches. The stitch size will vary according to the batting you use. If you want tiny stitches, choose a thin batting. If you are aiming for a high-loft look and strongly sculptured outlines for your patterns, choose a thicker batting and keep your stitches a consistent size. Larger stitches are now acceptable for certain forms of quilting.

Machine Quilting

Machine quilting presents a speedy alternative to hand quilting. Machines produce a wide variety of stitches and handle a variety of threads, both of which can enhance your quilting.

To machine quilt, fit your machine with a walking foot or use a machine with a dual-feed mechanism. Plan your stitching so you make as few starts as possible. Patterns that can be sewn in a single continuous line are particularly suitable for machine quilting.

You can use many different threads, including machine-embroidery thread, dressmaking thread, metallic and rayon threads, transparent nylon thread, and some quilting threads.

Before quilting, check your tension and stitch on a sample quilt sandwich made up of your chosen fabrics and batting. Adjust the tension so the top and bobbin threads lock inside the quilt sandwich and neither shows through to the other side.

For straight lines, set the machine for automatic stitching. For curves, set the machine on the slowest speed if you can. If your machine doesn't have this feature, set it for free-motion stitching and use your hands to guide the fabric through evenly. Meander quilting (page 93) is easiest to do with the machine set this way.

There are two ways to begin and end a line of machine quilting:

✦ Leave long thread ends. When you finish quilting, thread them onto a needle and tie them off on the underside as you would for hand quilting.

OR

✦ Lock the first and last stitches by taking a few stitches with the stitch length at zero. Trim the ends close to the quilt surface.

Machine Quilting with an Interfaced Backing

Despite careful basting, machine quilting can still cause the quilt top or backing to pucker. This can be solved by using a dense batting and replacing the backing fabric with a lightweight, fusible interfacing. The interfacing is ironed to one side of the batting, and the quilt top is basted to the other side. In effect, this produces two layers for quilting instead of three. It also leaves the smooth interfacing adjacent to the needle plate for ease of movement when quilting.

This method is ideal for pillow tops. For quilts, however, a fabric backing would need to be added after quilting. A further consideration is the long-term effects of the interfacing glue are unknown.

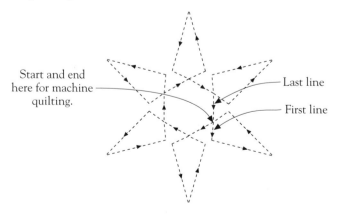

Start and end here for machine quilting.

Last line

First line

Machine Quilting Through Paper

This is one of my favourite machine-quilting techniques, especially for intricate patterns and hard-to-mark fabrics:

1. Trace the pattern onto lightweight tracing paper with a black marker.
2. Pin-baste the pattern to the quilt sandwich.
3. Machine quilt through all the layers, following the marked lines and working from the centre out.
4. Remove the tracing paper carefully so as not to pull stitches; use the blunt end of a seam ripper or your fingernails to remove small pieces of paper left in awkward areas.

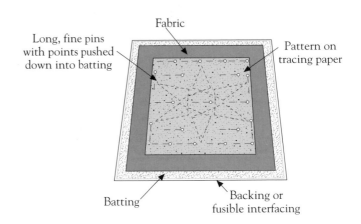

Fabric

Long, fine pins with points pushed down into batting

Pattern on tracing paper

Batting

Backing or fusible interfacing

Marking and Quilting Filler Patterns

❖ When marking straight-line filler patterns, it is important to keep the angles and line spacing correct. Lines of cross-hatching should intersect at 90°. Lines of diamond fill cross at 45° or 60°. Use a quilters' ruler with marked angles as a guide.

❖ Begin marking in the centre or widest part of the area to be filled. For cross-hatching and diamonds, draw two master lines, making sure they cross at the correct angle. Next, make tiny marks along each line at the correct intervals. Use these and your quilters' ruler to fill in the rest of the parallel lines.

For a filler of horizontal lines, draw one master line. Use your quilters' ruler to add parallel lines at the desired spacing.

❖ Masking tape can be used to mark the position of straight-line filler patterns. The tape is left in place while you stitch on one or both sides, then removed. Quilters' tape (¼"-wide masking tape) is useful for double lining both motifs and filler patterns with straight lines. Test the tape on the fabric first to check for damage or residue.

❖ Stipple quilting is done by hand and does not need to be marked. Begin in the centre or widest area of the space to be filled; avoid making consecutive stitches in the same direction.

❖ Meander and loop quilting are done by machine. Set the machine for free-motion stitching and keep the stitch length even. In meander quilting, do not cross over a previous line of stitching. (For more advice

on free-motion quilting, see Maurine Noble's *Machine Quilting Made Easy*, listed in the Bibliography.)

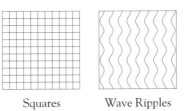

Squares   Wave Ripples   Cross-hatching

Horizontal Lines   Double Horizontal Lines   Diamonds

Stipple (hand quilting)

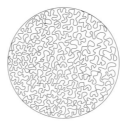

Meander (machine quilting)   Loops (machine quilting)

Bibliography

Bain, Iain. *Celtic Knotwork*. London, England: Constable, 1986.

Bridgewater, Alan and Gill. *Traditional & Folk Designs*. Tunbridge Wells, England: Search Press, 1990.

Chainey, Barbara. *The Essential Quilter*. Newton Abbot, England: David & Charles, 1993.

Cleland, Lee. *Quilting Makes the Quilt*. Bothell, Wash.: That Patchwork Place, 1994.

Davis, Courtney. *The Celtic Art Source Book*. London: Blandford Press, 1989.

Emms, Amy. *Amy Emms: The Story of Durham Quilting*. Tunbridge Wells, England: Search Press, 1990.

Finley, Ruth E. *Old Patchwork Quilts*. McLean, Va.: EPM Publications, 1929.

Fons, Marianne. *Fine Feathers: A Quilters' Guide to Customizing Traditional Feather Quilting Designs*. Lafayette, Calif.: C & T Publishing, 1988.

Jones, Owen. *The Grammar of Ornament*. London: Studio Editions, 1986 (first published 1856).

Kimball, Jeana. *Loving Stitches: A Guide to Fine Hand Quilting*. Bothell, Wash.: That Patchwork Place, 1992.

Le Roux, Charles. *Ornamentation Bretonne*. Nantes, France: Editions Reflets du Passe, 1984.

Noble, Maurine. *Machine Quilting Made Easy*. Bothell, Wash.: That Patchwork Place, 1994.

Osler, Dorothy. *Traditional British Quilts*. London: Batsford, 1987.

Osler, Dorothy. *Quilting*. London: Merehurst, 1991.

About the Author

During a working visit in the late 1960s to the American Museum in Bath, England, Dorothy Osler saw the wonderful quilt collection there and was inspired to take up quilting. At the time, she was working as "something completely different"—a geology curator at the Liverpool Museum.

In 1975, she moved back to her native Northeast England. The move prompted a change in career, and she became an active quilter, teacher, and writer. Increasingly, she began to specialise in quilting, in the strict sense, and quilt history. She is now recognised internationally as a leading authority on British quilt history.

Dorothy has been a member of the Quilters' Guild of Great Britain since its inception in 1979. She served on the national Executive Committee for six years as its first Heritage Officer. She is also a member of the American Quilt Study Group. She has taught in the United States and Canada, as well as throughout Britain and Europe. Her quilts have appeared in many exhibitions since the late 1970s, and she is also a respected exhibition juror. She has published three previous quilting books and numerous magazine articles worldwide, including in the United States and Japan.

Dorothy lives in Newcastle upon Tyne with her husband, a maritime historian. She has one grown daughter. When time allows, she and her husband love sailing their classic yacht.

Pattern Index